Under the Sea

Corals

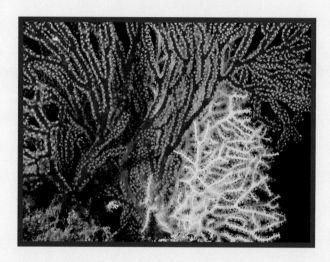

by Carol K. Lindeen

Consulting Editor: Gail Saunders-Smith, PhD
Consultant: Jody Rake, Member
Southwest Marine/Aquatic Educators' Association

Capstone
press

Mankato, Minnesota

Pebble Plus is published by Capstone Press,
151 Good Counsel Drive, P.O. Box 669, Mankato, Minnesota 56002.
www.capstonepress.com

1 2 3 4 5 6 10 09 08 07 06 05

Library of Congress Cataloging-in-Publication Data
Lindeen, Carol K., 1976–
    Corals / by Carol K. Lindeen.
    p. cm.—(Pebble Plus—Under the Sea)
    Includes bibliographical references and index.
    ISBN 0-7368-3660-8 (hardcover)
    1. Corals—Juvenile literature. I. Title. II. Series.
QL377.C5L56 2005
593.6—dc22   2004011097

Summary: Simple text and photographs present corals, their body parts, and their behavior.

Editorial Credits
Martha E. H. Rustad, editor; Juliette Peters, set designer; Kate Opseth, book designer; Kelly Garvin,
    photo researcher; Scott Thoms, photo editor

Photo Credits
Brand X Pictures/Keith Eskanos, 1
Jeff Rotman, 8–9, 12–13, 14–15
Minden Pictures/Chris Newbert, cover
Seapics.com/Mark Strickland, 6–7; Chris Newbert, 16–17; Mark Conlin, 18–19, 20–21
Steve Fabian, Phoenix, AZ, 11
Tom Stack & Associates Inc./Dave Fleetham, 4–5

Note to Parents and Teachers

The Under the Sea set supports national science standards related to the diversity and unity of life. This book describes and illustrates corals. The images support early readers in understanding the text. The repetition of words and phrases helps early readers learn new words. This book also introduces early readers to subject-specific vocabulary words, which are defined in the Glossary section. Early readers may need assistance to read some words and to use the Table of Contents, Glossary, Read More, Internet Sites, and Index sections of the book.

Table of Contents

What Are Corals?

Corals are sea animals.
They can look like colorful
fans or leaves.

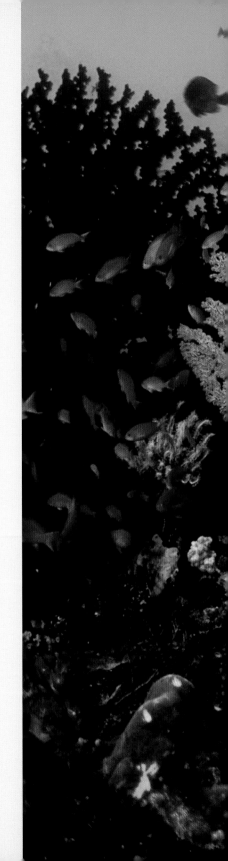

Two kinds of corals live under the sea. Hard corals grow in sheets. Soft corals have branches that sway in the water.

hard coral

soft coral

Corals live in groups

called colonies.

Each colony has

many corals.

9

Body Parts

Coral bodies are shaped
like tubes. Corals have
mouths at the end
of the tubes.

mouth

Corals have tentacles around their mouths. The tentacles sting small animals. Corals eat the animals.

tentacle

Some corals have
hard outer skeletons
shaped like cups.
Corals pull their bodies
inside the cups to stay safe.

Coral Reefs

Dead corals leave behind
old skeletons. These skeletons
make up coral reefs.
New corals grow
on coral reefs.

Coral reefs are found
in warm, shallow water.

Coral reefs can be very big.

Under the Sea

Corals live and grow
under the sea.

Glossary

branch—a part of a soft coral that grows out like an arm

colony—a large group of animals that live together

coral reef—an area of coral skeletons and rocks in shallow ocean water

shallow—not deep

skeleton—a structure that supports and protects the soft body of an animal; some corals have hard outer skeletons.

sting—to hurt with a small, sharp point; corals sting small animals with their tentacles.

sway—to move from side to side

tentacle—a thin, flexible arm on some animals; corals have tentacles around their mouths.

tube—a long cylinder, shaped like a soda can

Read More

Earle, Sylvia A. *Coral Reefs.* Jump into Science. Washington, D.C.: National Geographic, 2003.

Llewellyn, Claire. *Coral Reefs.* Geography Starts. Chicago: Heinemann Library, 2000.

Stone, Lynn M. *Corals.* Science Under the Sea. Vero Beach, Fla.: Rourke, 2003.

Internet Sites

FactHound offers a safe, fun way to find Internet sites related to this book. All of the sites on FactHound have been researched by our staff.

Here's how:

1. Visit *www.facthound.com*

2. Type in this special code **0736836608** for age-appropriate sites. Or enter a search word related to this book for a more general search.

3. Click on the **Fetch It** button.

FactHound will fetch the best sites for you!

Index

Word Count: 133
Grade Level: 1
Early-Intervention Level: 14